MACH 4®
Mental Training System

Tennis Handbook and Workbook II for Coaches, Parents, and Players

Anne Smith, Ph.D.

MACH 4® Mental Training System Tennis Handbook and Workbook II for Coaches, Parents, and Players
Anne Smith, Ph.D.
Copyright 2008 Anne Smith, Inc.
All rights reserved

MACH 4® Mental Training System
All rights reserved. Permission is granted to the buyer of this Workbook to photocopy worksheets as long as the Copyright at the bottom of the Worksheets remains. Otherwise, no part of this publication may be reproduced or transmitted in any form or by any means, electronic or mechanical, including photocopying, recording, or any information storage or retrieval system without written permission from the publisher.

Published by Team Alf Books
Phoenix, Arizona

Phone: 480-272-5085
Fax: 480-214-5232

ISBN 0-9778958-5-4

Email: anne@annesmithtennis.com
www.annesmithtennis.com

Cover and Interior Design by Sential Design
www.sentialdesign.com

Additional Resources by Anne Smith:
MACH 4® Mental Training System A Handbook for Athletes, Coaches and Parents
GRAND SLAM: Coach Your Mind to Win in Sports, Business, and Life
MACH 4® Mental Training System Tennis Workbook

MACH 4®
Mental Training System

TABLE OF CONTENTS

HANDBOOK

SECTION ONE – Worksheets for Coaches and Parents

    I.   Short-Term and Long-Term Goals Worksheets

    II.   Philosophy and Mission Statement Worksheet

    III.   Emotional Goals Worksheet

    IV.   Body Language Goals Worksheet

    V.   Best Intensity Level Worksheet

    VI.   Before-Matches Worksheet

    VII.   During-Matches Worksheet

    VIII.   After-Matches Worksheet

    IX.   Match Summary Worksheet

    X.   Progress Report Worksheet

    XI.   Daily Point Worksheet

    XII.   Match and Post-Match Intensity Level Worksheets

    XIII.   Free Points & Cueing Worksheet

SECTION TWO – Worksheets for Players

- I. Short-Term and Long-Term Goals Worksheets
- II. Emotional Goals Worksheet
- III. Body Language Goals Worksheet
- IV. Best Intensity Level Worksheet
- V. Cueing Language Worksheet - Technique
- VI. Game Plan Worksheet
- VII. Match Request Worksheet
- VIII. Before-Matches Worksheet
- IX. During-Matches Worksheet
- X. After-Matches Worksheet
- XI. Match Summary Worksheet
- XII. Progress Report Worksheet
- XIII. Post-Match Intensity Level Worksheet
- XIV. Tennis Questionnaire

MACH 4®
Mental Training System

Handbook

Handbook

The MACH 4® Mental Training System Tennis Handbook and Workbook II for Coaches, Parents, and Players was created to be a supplement to my book titled "MACH 4® Mental Training System: A Handbook for Athletes, Coaches and Parents." In addition to the worksheets for players in my book, I have included an overview of the MACH 4® System, examples of how to apply the System during practices and matches, and worksheets for coaches and parents in this Handbook/Workbook. MACH 4® is a simple, effective system that provides organization and structure for tennis programs and tennis families by teaching coaches and parent's effective ways to dialogue with their players/children, conduct practice sessions, and create a winning team.

A critical component that is missing from tennis is the philosophy of building a winning team between coaches, parents, and players. Coaches, parents, and players must all work together to achieve a common goal. Demonstrating caring, effective, and empowering communication with your players/children is the best way to teach and inspire them. Coaches and parents must work together and think of themselves as being on the same team. Coaches need to involve parents by including them in the process, rather than excluding them. This being said, there are certain guidelines that need to be followed by all parties involved; including players, to ensure respectful and empowering relationships that produce the best results. It is all about dialogue and delivery – knowing what to say, when to say it, and; most importantly, how to say it.

Bev Raws, James Jack, and I use the MACH 4® System every day at our tennis academy in Paradise Valley, Arizona to build a winning team between coaches, parents, and players. Our Academy runs Monday through Thursday 4pm to 6pm with 7-year-old to 16-year-old male and female tournament players. We believe that the MACH 4® System has positively impacted not only our players' performance, but also their behavior and relationships with each other and their parents. Our parents have benefited from the MACH 4® System because they are learning effective ways to dialogue with their children and to bring out the best in them.

The role of coaches and parents is to determine the best ways to enhance their player's/child's performance and behavior. Players need a strong, supportive team to help them produce winning results. We are all on the player's/child's team, not the other way around. No one should be on the player's/child's team who is not providing the best support and means to help the player/child perform their best. We have found that by using the MACH 4® System to build a strong teamwork between coaches, parents, and players; everyone is happier, our players enjoy the game more, there is less tension and anxiety, practices are more efficient and productive, and our players are improving more rapidly and are achieving better results sooner rather than later.

My coach, Bev Raws, and I developed the MACH 4® Mental Training System as a result of my comeback to the women's professional tennis tour, beginning in January 2005. As Bev and I traveled to tournaments, it became more and more obvious to us the importance of the mental part of the game. When I first started back on the tour, we initially focused on making some changes in my movement. But we soon realized that my mindset before, during, and after my matches was more important than the technical part of the game.

I was being featured in my singles matches, and I had not played on the tour for 14 years! I was *very* nervous and had no confidence in my game. Right before my match against Stephanie Dubois (ranked top 200 in the world) in Midland, Michigan, Bev said, "Just fake it. Pretend it is 1982, and you are #1 in the world in doubles and #12 in the world in singles. Act confident no matter what. If you miss, act like it doesn't bother you." It worked! That was the beginning of the development of the MACH 4® system.

Bev has coached tennis for more than 25 years, so her expertise and approach to the game helped me to be successful again on the tour. My goals were to understand the "modern game" and to win one more doubles title. I am happy to say, I accomplished both. My new mental approach helped me to improve more quickly and easily. I incorporated the MACH 4® system into my game, and it dramatically improved my performance. We have taken what we learned from my year-and-a-half return to the Tour, applied it to club-level players, world-ranked juniors, nationally ranked juniors, tour players, and players and parents at our Academy, and expanded it to provide tennis programs and tennis families with an organized, structured framework that produces winning results.

I will briefly describe the components of the MACH 4® System and then provide examples of how we apply the System to our Academy, including guidelines, the mission statement, code of conduct, and our coaching philosophy. MACH 4® can also be applied to junior clinics and private lessons. Please read my book titled "MACH 4® Mental Training System: A Handbook for Athletes, Coaches and Parents" for a more comprehensive look at the four components of the MACH 4® System.

Why call the System MACH 4®? The MACH 4® Mental Training System consists of four components: mental, body language, intensity level, and cueing language. Combining these four components will help coaches, parents, and players reach their goals "faster than the speed of sound." All of the components are interrelated and work together to create a positive partnership with the mind and the body to ensure maximum performance. In order to achieve this, the mind and the body have to be trained to work together as a team. I will now describe each component.

1) Mental Component - the mental component involves how a player thinks about their match before they walk on the court, what they say to themselves during the match, and what they choose to focus on during the match. Additional examples of the mental part of tennis are: how a player chooses to carry themselves on the court, how they choose to react to missed shots, how they choose to react to what they think are bad line calls, having a game plan, shot selection, staying with

winning play patterns, maintaining their best intensity level, and what they and their coach or parent choose to focus on after the match. The mental component of tennis is what a coach, parent, or player can say and do to create the least amount of pressure on the player so that they can perform.

2) Body Language Component - body language will energize a player. From the moment a player arrives at a tennis tournament, their body language, how they carry themselves, is paramount. **As a player, do you project a confident, fighter image? Do you walk with a spring in your step, your head held high, and your shoulders back? How do you walk onto the court?** A player can use their body language to intimidate their opponent before the match even begins and to keep their own nerves at bay. That is the magic of MACH 4® – no matter who the opponent is or how they are performing, a player can project confidence with their own actions so that energy/intensity levels remain strong and concentrated rather than being wasted or given away to the opponent. It is easy to train, and it is a choice.

Coaches and parents are also responsible for their body language and how they act while watching their player/child perform. **Do you appear calm and confident or are you giving your player/child signals and clapping for the opponent's mistakes? Are you courteous and respectful to other coaches, parents, players, and officials?** The manner in which coaches and parents choose to conduct themselves while attending tournaments will have a significant impact on their player/child. It can make or break the next match or tournament. To ensure successful results, make sure your body language and conduct always have a positive, empowering impact.

3) Intensity Level Component - it is so important to recognize physical responses to match moments. Intensity level has to do with not only a physical feeling but with footwork and how hard a player swings at the ball. Another way to think about intensity level is hand speed or racquet head acceleration. Intensity level does **not** mean for a player to be intense or to have tight muscles.

In the MACH 4® System, we rate intensity level on a scale from 1-5. For example, 1-2 = low intensity; 3-4 = medium intensity; and 5 = high intensity. A player needs to have their best intensity level during their match in order to produce the best results. If a player's intensity level is either too low or too high, then their game will suffer. Intensity level has the potential to fluctuate based on the score, how a player perceives they are hitting the ball, how they are feeling, etc. The goal is for a player to be aware of and monitor their intensity level in order to keep it within a specific range so that it does not fluctuate wildly during their matches. Fluctuations in intensity levels cause problems. For example, if a player is serving for the match and their intensity level decreases (e.g., hand speed slows down) from a 4 to a 2, it is very likely that they will not perform their best that game. When a player slows their hand down on their serve, the pace of their serve decreases and this gives the opponent the opportunity to hit a better return. We coach our players to swing at the ball with a 3.5 or 4 intensity level on their ground strokes with an occasional 5 intensity level. We do not recommend using a 5 intensity level on match points! We coach them to use a 4.5 or 5 intensity level on their first serve. We discovered

that if they lowered their intensity level on their first serve, then their ground strokes also lowered to the same intensity level.

Remember to individualize intensity level to your player's style and technique. A level 4 on one player's serve will be different than a level 4 on another player's serve. The nice thing about intensity level is that it is completely within a player's control, and it is critical for a winning performance. Once players take responsibility for their intensity level, then they will have a better opportunity to play their best and win.

We often give our players MACH 4® quizzes as homework assignments. One question on MACH 4® Quiz #1 was **"Does your opponent have anything to do with you playing at your best intensity level? Why?"** One of our 9-year-old females gave the following answer, "No, because my opponent does not affect my game. I am the only one who is in control of my game". Another question was **"What would cause you to not play with your best intensity level for the entire match?"** She answered, "Slow feet, thinking about other things, worrying about what other people think of me, and slow racket speed." This young girl has good awareness and is well on her way to taking responsibility for her own game and her own intensity level.

Intensity level can also be applied to footwork. The intensity level on my footwork used to be about a 4 until Bev pointed out that I needed to lower the intensity level on my footwork; my feet where moving too fast, and this was zapping my energy. I lowered my intensity level on my footwork to about a 3 and found that I moved more smoothly to the ball, I was in better position to hit the ball, I did not get as tired, and I had more spin and pace on my shots. I found out that having too high of an intensity level on my footwork was causing the intensity level on my swing to slow down. Again, intensity level needs to be individualized or personalized to the player. Some of the students I teach have too low of an intensity level on their footwork, so they need to bump it up to a 3.5 or 4. It all starts with the intensity level of the feet.

Intensity level applies to coaches and parents as well. It is critical to be aware of your own intensity level during interactions with others. **What is your best intensity level when talking? What is your best intensity level when watching your player/child during practices and tournaments?** One of our parents said his intensity level had been MACH 10. Now, he keeps his intensity level at a 2 and sits back in his chair. This change in his intensity level helps his children to remain calm and confident. **What is your best intensity level when interacting with your player/child after a match?** I heard a story about a young girl who was crying when she went to report her score. The official thought that she had lost her match. The young girl won; but was greeted by her coach after the match and angrily told about all of the "mistakes" she had made. **How long do you think she will stay in the game? Is it a wonder why we have lost so many talented players before they could realize their potential?** It is our responsibility as coaches and parents to ensure that our intensity level and dialogue has a positive, empowering impact on our players at all times. It is critical to a child's happiness and success.

4) Cueing Language Component - cueing language is words or phrases that can trigger certain mental, emotional, visual, and physical responses. Cueing language can be used in a variety of ways. One way is for players to develop cues or phrases for their own self-talk or internal dialogue. For example, when I say "next point," this helps me to re-set for the next point so that I am not thinking about the point I just played. Cueing language helps me to stay in the moment.

Cueing language can also be used to enhance technique. It is important for players to have cues to use during matches on each of their strokes. For example, my cue on my serve is "acceleration." This cue helps me to keep my hand moving at a 5 intensity level on my serve. On my FH it is "racquet face down." Cueing language is a great way to incorporate mental training with technique because it teaches players constructive ways to deal with misses. Using cues helps to eliminate emotional reactions associated with misses. The focus shifts from emotionally judging missed shots that disrupts concentration to positive cueing that improves performance.

I have also found cueing to be helpful not only with my own tennis, but with players that I teach at all levels of the game. Coaches can use cueing language by developing certain terms or phrases that are descriptive of specific shots and situations; and then teach the technique involved in the shot. For example, Bev and I have coined a shot called the "meatball." The meatball is one of the most difficult shots in the game. It is that high, slow ball that a player volleys. It is a high ball with no pace on it, and it usually happens on the third or fourth shot in doubles. The player either hits it in the back fence or the bottom of the net. They will usually say, **"I can't believe I missed that shot. It was so easy."** Most players do not give the meatball enough attention, precisely because they think it is so easy. The keys to hitting the meatball are to move to the ball with your feet first (rather than standing and taking a big swing), to keep your chin up and look at the ball, to have a short follow-through, and to aim for the service line. Once a coach has explained the technique involved in a shot, and the player understands the technical way to hit the shot, the coach only needs to cue them with a word or phrase without going into lengthy discussions every time. It helps to keep things simple and fun. It also adds humor to practices. When players are less anxious, their muscles remain more relaxed which enables them to execute their shots.

Cueing language can and should also be individualized. A cue that works for one player might not work for another. It is important for coaches, parents, and players to come up with cues that are meaningful for them. Martina Navratilova loved the cueing language I used with her when I coached her during the 2005 and 2006 World Team Tennis Boston Lobsters season. She liked Chunky Monkey and First Strike. She even coined her own cue, Slender Monkey. Hey, if it is good enough for Martina, it is certainly good enough for the rest of us!

All of the MACH 4® components working together will produce focus and concentration. Players cannot just have positive self-talk and a low intensity level and play well. When players keep a positive mindset, display strong body language, maintain their best intensity level, and use meaningful cueing language, they will automatically focus. Think of this winning MACH 4® formula:

**Strong mindset + Strong body language + Best intensity level
+ Positive cueing language = Automatic focus**

The following examples are provided to demonstrate how we apply the MACH 4® System to our Academy. Our guidelines, the mission statement, code of conduct, and our coaching philosophy are summarized below.

1) Establish Guidelines – the coach sets the tone. The coach must have a coaching philosophy, create standards or a code of conduct for parents and players, and develop a mission statement. When there are no guidelines, there is an increased chance for confusion, disorganization, and unacceptable behavior.

The Mission of Rasta-Smith Tennis Academy (RSTA) is to develop independent individuals who are Champions on and off the court, and to create empowering partnerships between coaches, parents, and players. To accomplish this mission, all parents and players must be on board with the philosophy of the Academy. One item in our Code of Conduct is that no player has a guaranteed "spot" at RSTA. Participating in the Academy must be valued by parents and players as well. The Academy requires that parents and players embrace and implement the concepts and philosophy of the Academy. They are to represent RSTA and themselves well; both behaviorally and verbally during practices and tournaments.

2) Parents are on the Team – we do not exclude parents. This would just cause more problems. We encourage parents to be involved, based on the established guidelines that we have set. We invite them to come onto the court during practice (with the guideline of no commenting or talking to their child or to other parents while on-court. Their children also know they must not interact with their parents or their parents cannot stay and learn). Parents can listen to us and know exactly what is being taught and how it is being communicated. This allows parents to understand exactly what we are focusing on with their child so they can reinforce what is being taught with the lingo or phrasing that is being used. We encourage questions and give explanations as needed.

When parents do not want to be a part of our program or System that we have established, or to follow the guidelines; they communicate this through their actions. When parents choose to not be on the team, which is really their child's team, not theirs, then there really is no point in having their child in our academy. What we teach will surely be "deep-sixed" since we are with the children such a small percentage of the time. The parents we currently have at our Academy have seen the benefits and positive results of following the MACH 4® system within a short period of time.

3) Demand Ethical Behavior and Good Sportsmanship at all Times – this starts with coaches and parents. It is our responsibility to teach and educate players regarding acceptable, fair, and ethical behavior. Cheating should never be encouraged or condoned. Coaches, parents, and players must realize that winning in tennis is not a life-or-death matter. When coaches and parents act as if winning a tennis match were a life-or-death matter; they put additional anxiety and tension on their players/children. Temptation to win at all costs may include cheating by

making bad line calls, taking too long in-between points, signaling or coaching a player/child to take a bathroom break so you can talk to them, etc. In addition, coaches and parents should never coach their players/children during tournament play from the sidelines with verbal or visual cues. This is cheating; it is not helping your player/child to be independent. It is giving them the message that they are not good enough to play and win on their own.

Cheating is not tolerated at our Academy or during tournaments. We teach our players to be respectful to other players and officials. It is important to play fairly and to engage umpires or officials by speaking with respect rather than alienating them by disrespectful behavior or rude comments. A parent or player is much more likely to get the benefit of the doubt from an official when they are respectful.

4) Have Team Meetings - meetings that provide a forum for give-and-take between coaches, parents, and players are necessary to keep the team strong. Communication is a two-way street. When players hear only the coach's or parent's dialogue and are not given an opportunity to respond, they are likely to tune out and shut down. We begin every practice with a MACH 4® meeting. In this meeting, we ask the players questions or quiz them about the MACH 4® System that we implement every day in practice. This reinforces what they are learning, and it gives us feedback about how they are interpreting things in their minds. We do not assume that they understand everything we say, so we consistently ask them what they think. This lets them know they are an important part of the team, and we learn from them as well.

5) Dialogue and Delivery – this is what one says and the manner in which it is said. This includes body language, tone of voice, intensity level, and content. Before reacting to a situation, we think about the ramifications of what we will say to parents and players. When a parent is critical or unhappy with something, we consider what we should say and how we should say it to them in order to achieve the best results and create a win-win situation. When a player is not practicing at their best intensity level or not doing what is required, we take a few minutes to determine what we could say to inspire them, rather than alienate or demoralize them. We give them choices. **"Are you too tired to hit with your best intensity? If so, why don't you rest for a few minutes?"** Every child we have said this to during practice has responded the same way, **"No, I am not tired. I do not need to sit down and rest."** We respond with **"Well then, go back out there and bump it up."** When given choices and not commands, they make positive choices.

In addition, sarcasm is not allowed. We do not make fun of nor embarrass our players. We do not permit them to be sarcastic or tease each other. Sarcasm and public displays of criticism are negative. Negativity breeds anger, resentment, and frustration. These emotions and feelings create undo stress that may lead to injury, illness, or nonperformance, not to mention players never wanting to play tennis again. We have high standards at our academy; but there is not one child who is not having fun when this atmosphere is maintained. We provide our players with positive feedback on what they are doing well. When we talk to them after their matches, our first comment is **"Tell us everything you did well."**

6) Speak with Respect – we do not shout at our players or speak in a harsh, disrespectful manner to them. We require the same from them. We require our players to say **"hello" and "goodbye"** and to say **"thank you"** to the coaches after every practice. When we give our players feedback about shot selection, intensity level, spin on the ball, behavior, or certain play patterns; we require them to stop, to look at us, to listen, and to acknowledge what we are telling them by saying **"okay"** or giving a **"thumbs up"**. This helps to teach players to be respectful and to appreciate and to value the coach's input and time. Nothing should be taken for granted. Respect and appreciation raise self-esteem and confidence.

7) Ban the Words "mistake" and "error" – these are such powerful, negative words. The brain latches on to them and will keep a player fearful. If the focus is always on "mistakes" or "errors," then players will keep making the same ones over and over. These words trigger a vicious cycle of negativity and nonperformance. We have replaced the word "mistake" with the word "miss". Nobody tries to miss. When we dialogued this concept to our players, it was as if the weight of the world had been lifted off of their shoulders. They told us they were no longer afraid to hit the ball. This is how powerful words are in a moment to performance. Players will either make it or miss it. We do not comment on or react emotionally to misses. We comment on intensity level, body language, cueing language, and shot selection. This helps to keep their technique strong.

Another strategy we use is to focus on what our players are doing well. For example, when our players try something in practice that we have been working on, we specifically comment right then, **"I liked the way you moved to the short ball"** or **"I like the amount of spin you put on that ball."** When we focus on what our players are doing well, we can literally see a physical reaction or change in body language (e.g., smile, stand up taller, look proud). By focusing and commenting on what they are doing well, we are encouraging them, positively reinforcing what we want them to do; therefore, increasing the likelihood that they will repeat that behavior.

8) Create a Safe Environment – as mentioned above, we do not use the words "mistake" or "error." We do not talk about winning or losing with our players. Instead, we focus on creating an environment for our players to take risks and learn new things. Wanting to win is a given. Our players want to win and they believe they can win. We want our players to win. Their parents want their children to win. However, when the primary focus is on winning, this just creates more tension, stress, and anxiety for everyone, particularly the player. This often results in a loss. We always focus on the basics (intensity level, body language, cueing language, spin, and play patterns) in addition to teaching new shots and strategies. When we do this, our players have more fun, improve, and develop more tools to win. We create this environment by complimenting them when they try something new and focusing on the attempt not the outcome. We ask them to use what we are teaching them in practice in their tournament matches. When the primary focus is on the basics and learning new shots and strategies, the winning will take care of itself.

9) Accept Accolades – we teach our players to accept positive feedback and compliments graciously. We do this because unfortunately, many people are negative based and are looking to make negative comments thinking that this will help their players perform better. This style of coaching never inspired me to play my best. It only added more anxiety and fear. We do not reinforce our players with harsh comments or punishment such as running laps or doing push-ups. Push-ups on a cement court are not safe for any child to do. Players that respond to negative coaching or parenting may not allow themselves to win. Some players, who have been reinforced with negative feedback, may choose to lose just so they can continue to receive negative feedback from their coach or parents. Or, they are so afraid to miss a shot because they are thinking about what their coach or parent will say to them after the match. When this happens, players cannot implement what they have been training in practice. It is a vicious cycle. **Why take a chance?** We teach our players to accept positive feedback and to say **"thank you"** when receiving a compliment. This helps them to be stronger inside which is what they need to perform at their best. When they can accept accolades and applaud their own shots rather than dwell on their misses, then they have chosen the best game plan to win.

10) Abide by the Ten Minute Rule - coaches and parents, please allow yourself and your player time to decompress after a match; particularly after a loss! We allow at least ten minutes to pass before discussing the match with our players. This does not preclude, of course, congratulating them after a win. The ten minutes gives them a chance to go to the referee's desk, to the restroom, to get a drink of water, and to emotionally recover enough to be able to talk about their match. We first ask them to tell us what they think they did well during the match. We do this because coaches and parents often put too much emotion into winning or losing, rather than maintaining some distance from the emotional aspect. The first impulse for some coaches and parents is to point out everything the player did wrong; this is not effective at all. Most players are already too hard on themselves so they do not need coaches or parents adding to that; we need to lessen it! One of our players told us that she had broken four racquets before training at our Academy. Since coming to our Academy and being coached with the MACH 4® System, she has not broken another one and she is proud of it! We also do not want our players to come off of the court afraid or fearful of what we will say to them. Based on what our players tell us about what they think they did well during the match, when necessary; we ask them what they think they will need to do differently in their next match.

11) Increase Awareness – to achieve this, we have created the MACH 4® Mental Training System Daily Point Worksheet, a daily point and bonus point system using the MACH 4® components of body language and intensity level. We rate our players each practice on a scale from 1 to 5 regarding their body language and intensity level during drills and point play. After practice is over each day, the players run to get their notebooks with their point sheets. They love to receive points. Receiving points has made them more aware of their body language and best intensity levels. They work as a team to redeem their points for rewards. We set the award amount and equate it to airline frequent flyer rewards. This teaches them that every point matters. Each player must have a certain amount of points

per month to remain in our academy. They also earn what they receive. We would never just give them an article of clothing to wear with our Academy's name on it. They earn it through their dedication and work ethic, just like some of us did in high school when we earned our letter jackets. They will appreciate it, value it, and wear it with pride.

12) Practice IS Important – too many players discount practice. One professional player I have worked with used to believe that practice was not important. I asked her, **"Then why do you practice so much?"** I often ask players, **"What is the difference between practice and a match?"** They always reply, **"Pressure. Matches count."** I then say, **"The only difference between practice and a match is in your mind."** No wonder players who think like that get so nervous in their matches. They count! If a player thinks that practices do not count, then they are less likely to practice with strong body language, positive cueing language, and their best intensity level. The way I look at it is if players practice with their best intensity level, strong body language, and positive cueing language, then when they play a tournament, they will be much more likely to implement these components in match play. Our players know, MACH 4® first; then begin the point. Every ball they hit in practice is valued. They do not want to chance hitting a ball with a 1-2 intensity level that could change the outcome of a match. This philosophy helps them to achieve their goals sooner rather than later. When a player is constantly practicing the MACH 4® System, they improve faster. We teach our players that practices are just as important as matches and that there should be no difference in their minds between practices and tournaments. When we do drills and then play points, we make sure their intensity level does not drop just because they are playing points. This mindset and training has produced more enjoyment and winning tournament results.

13) Stay on Track – do not go off on tangents. The benefit of using the MACH® System is that it helps to keep coaches, parents, and players organized and structured. Too many times I hear coaches, parents, and players going off on tangents, such as **"My player is just making too many mistakes,"** **"I don't mind when my child loses to an opponent who pushes the ball because that game is not going to take them very far,"** **"I lost because my opponent hit the ball too soft,"** etc. This type of thinking and dialoguing can cause delays in a player's/child's tennis development.

When coaches, parents, and players utilize the MACH 4® System, the predominant style of thinking and manner of dialoguing about practices and matches is focused on mindset, body language, intensity level, and cueing language. Almost all feedback is based on these components. The advantage of using the MACH 4® System is that coaches, parents, and players are speaking the same language. Speaking a common language is critical because we are not always available to watch our players compete in tournaments. Parents are the ones traveling to watch their children play. When we debrief over the phone with a parent or player after a match, the discussion is centered on body language, positive cueing, and intensity level. This keeps everyone on the same page and leads to faster improvements in the player's/child's game.

14) Tennis is Not Just About Forehands and Backhands - tennis is not just about technique. With all things being equal, a player's mindset will determine the outcome of the match. It comes down to the player who is able to control their emotions and reactions to external factors that determines the end result. It is about a player's ability to control their emotions and reactions when they are not hitting the ball cleanly or exactly like they want. It is about their ability to respond positively when things are not going as planned. It is about managing moodiness, irritability, frustration, anger, fear, anxiety, perfectionism, missed opportunities, bad line calls, the wind, heat, and/or sun, bad lights, a sweaty grip, not getting to practice what they want to when they want to, frustrations, flight delays, long car trips to tournaments, being upset with their parents or coach before a match, traveling, hotels, eating out, being sore or injured, rain delays, the crucial moments of a match, playing against an opponent they do not particularly like, playing against their doubles partner, being the #1 seed, playing against the #1 seed, their opponent's comments during the match, bathroom breaks or injury timeouts, not knowing the exact time they will play their match, losing, a noisy crowd, an umpire who is weak and indecisive, a lines person who continues to make questionable calls, not being able to practice as much as they think they need to, jet lag, having never beaten their current opponent, having always beaten their current opponent, playing someone ranked much lower, playing someone ranked much higher, playing on their least favorite surface, changing grips, changing coaches, playing doubles with someone they do not like, being tired, a racquet strung too tight or too loose, breaking a string on their favorite racquet right before a match, playing against someone who hits the ball soft, playing against someone who hits the ball hard, etc. **Have I missed anything?** Compared to all of this, just focusing on technique is easy! At our Academy we have MACH 4® meetings to discuss and address these issues and possible scenarios. This helps give our players confidence going into matches. They will know what to do and how to handle these situations if/when they arise.

15) Do Not Discount Your Opponent – do not take your opponent for granted. More often than not, when players do not respect their opponents, they do not play with their best intensity level and most of the time they end up losing the match, precisely because they thought they were so much better than their opponent. Thoughts and words like the following add more "pressure" not less. **"My first round opponent is terrible. Who do I play in the second round?" "This will be an easy match. I have never lost to this guy." "He's a human backboard. I'll just go out and hit winners."** This type of thinking backfires most of the time. When I hear these types of comments, I know there may be a problem. The players who have said these things to me then go on to tell me how they think they lost these matches, when in reality, it all started with their thoughts before the match. The mind will always control physical response.

It is very important for coaches, parents, and players to have a healthy respect for all opponents no matter what they are ranked. I was always ranked #1 in Texas in my age group and the age group above me. I often beat opponents 6-0, 6-0. Even if I had previously beaten an opponent 6-0, 6-0, I never took her for granted or went into the next match against her thinking **"this will be easy."** My father instilled

this philosophy in me. It taught me to be respectful to others and to always be prepared to play my best.

16) Stick with Play Patterns – do not deviate. Too many players have no strategy or game plan. They appear to be mindlessly hitting the ball from corner to corner or even down the middle with no rhyme or reason. We coach our players to have a play pattern and to stick with it. For example, we encourage our players to hit the majority of their balls crosscourt, wait for the shorter ball they can step into, hit it down the line, come to net, and volley short crosscourt. This one play pattern alone made our players stronger immediately.

Play patterns are helpful for many reasons. First, they give a player structure and purpose. Second, they help a player feel more confident and less edgy because they have a specific plan to follow. Third, they improve consistency and patience and encourage higher percentage tennis. Fourth, they can frustrate and intimidate an opponent. When I watch matches, I often see players decide to change a winning game plan or winning play patterns, resulting in a loss. Unfortunately, they usually decide to change their play patterns when they are ahead and ready to close out the set or the match. This is not the time to experiment. This is the time to stay with what got you in a winning position. As my mother often says, **"Never change a winning game plan!"** The MACH 4® System is all about creating structure and organization. Play patterns are part of the System, and they do produce winning results.

17) Spin, Spin, Spin – more topspin is the answer for most players. We always tell our players that if they want to hit an intensity level 5, they have to put more spin on the ball. Otherwise, it will sail long most of the time. Hitting spin on the ball is critical for many reasons. First, spin gives a player more of a margin for safety. Second, spin increases a player's consistency level. Third, a ball hit with heavy spin has more bite or action on it; and it is much more difficult to return. Fourth, spin allows a player to hit lower bouncing balls with a higher intensity level. Fifth, spin gives a player more options by allowing them to hit more areas of the court. Sixth, spin allows a player to create sharper angles and pull their opponent out of the court. Coaching our players to hit with adequate spin on the ball is another vital part of the MACH 4® System – spin is the way to go. And believe me, they still hit the ball hard!

18) Manage Perfectionism – as I like to say, **"I'm a recovering perfectionist."** During my career, my perfectionism just fueled my anger so it never helped me to perform my best. When one thinks about it, it is ridiculous to set such standards for oneself. I have never seen a perfect tennis match. Even Roger Federer misses. It is how we handle those misses that will either keep us strong or derail our play. Trying to be perfect and never miss a ball is an impossible task. It only leads to frustration and playing too safe. It certainly makes it hard to enjoy the game we love. I have replaced that thinking with MACH 4®. It is definitely serving me well both on and off the court.

19) Champions Find a Way to Win – even when they are not playing their best. I often hear players of all levels say, **"I just wasn't feeling the ball today"** or **"I lost**

because I wasn't playing my best." In my career, I may have felt like I was hitting the ball really well and everything was flowing about one tournament a year. A player cannot always **"feel the ball"** or be comfortable with every shot all of the time. Players have to find a way to win no matter how they are feeling or playing on a given day. When a player thinks their strokes always have to feel great or they cannot win, then they will be frustrated, discouraged, and irritated about their game more often than not. Find a way to win even when things are not going your way. Stay determined. That is the true mark of a champion.

20) Allow Your Players/Children to Learn How to Win – too many coaches and parents have the philosophy that they do not care if their player/child wins at a younger age because they are developing their game for the future. They say things like, **"I don't mind when my child loses to an opponent who pushes the ball because that game is not going to take them very far."** (We have banned all forms of the word "push"). There is no need to demean another player's game, especially when they won the match. Attaching negativity to lobbing or hitting balls higher over the net is wrong. We teach our players ways to neutralize all shots that give them trouble. For example, we tell them, **"If the ball is slow, keep your best intensity level and move quickly to the ball. Slower balls do not mean that YOU go slower!"** I hear coaches and parents say, **"I want my player/child to hit the ball as hard as they can – win or lose."** This kind of thinking is not going to help your player/child learn how to win. It is important for players/children to take their current technical, physical, and mental skills and to figure out a way to win with what they have.

Some coaches and parents also encourage their players/children to play "up" in an older age group. This is also not teaching them how to win unless they are already ranked high in their age group; then playing up is warranted because they have learned how to win and their skill level has improved. It is very important for players to learn how to beat their peers. This is where the "pressure" is. It is not pressure to play up in another age group, especially two age groups up. That is much easier since they are not expected to win. I do not understand a particular game style outweighing accomplishment. Both can be achieved at the same time. We would rather see our players figure out ways to win, add more shots to their game, do well in their age group, and then transition into the next age group. Learning how to win is the most important skill of all. Allow your players/children to learn how to win while they are growing into new shots. **With this philosophy, how could your players/children not accomplish their goals?**

21) Be Strong from the Inside Out – we teach our players to be strong from within rather than relying on external factors for motivation. We want them to want to play and win for themselves. Coaches and parents cannot want their player/child to play tennis and win **more** than their player/child wants to play tennis and win. It is not about the parent wanting it more than the child. This does not work. This only creates unhappy players/children. We want our players to play for the love of the game and to enjoy the sport. It is up to us to make sure this happens.

Of course we want our players to win, but the motivation to play and to train and to do what it takes to become a champion must come from within them. We tell

our players that we are not there in practice to motivate them. Our players have to choose to motivate themselves. That is why it is important for coaches and parents to not encourage their players to look over at them during practices or matches for motivation. When I played, I rarely if ever needed my parents or my coach to clap and yell for me to **"Come on!"** I got that from within. Also, looking around detracts from performance. If our players choose to look over at us or their parents during matches, then they do so when they have done something well; rather than always looking over when they are struggling or losing. When they do this, I often wonder in that moment if they want us to come in and play for them. We train them in practice sessions to keep their eyes within the court. The tennis court has the same shape as their cell phone. We say to them, **"Please give your match the same focus and intensity that you give your cell phone when you are text messaging each other"**. Players can hear clapping or whatever they have asked their coach/parent/friends/ to do to help them without constantly looking over to those watching to save the day. Players must be strong from within, and we must teach them how. They need to rely on themselves and believe they can do it whether their coach and/or parents are there to watch them or not. Champions are strong from the inside out.

The goal of this MACH 4® Handbook and Workbook is to make coaches, parents, and players more aware of thoughts, emotions, and behaviors that hold them back so that necessary changes can be made to produce the best results. By reading this Handbook and completing the worksheets, coaches and parents will understand what they need to say and how they need to act in order to bring out the best in themselves and their player/child; document improvements in their player's/child's game and behavior; and be aware of and acknowledge even the smallest progress made in their player's/child's game. We have noticed that coaches and parents sometimes forget how far their players/children have come. Completing these worksheets will help to remind them to celebrate and reinforce even the smallest improvement in their player's/child's game and behavior before saying, "Yes, but…. they need to do this, this, and this."

By completing these worksheets, players will understand what they need from their coach and parent(s) and know precisely what they need to do to consistently keep their best intensity level and win. Most importantly, by implementing MACH 4® off-the-court and on-the-court during practices, lessons, and matches, coaches, parents, and players will create a winning team that produces better relationships and winning results. Our players continually tell us that MACH 4® is something that they can feel and count on to help them to win. It makes their technique stronger. They have also said that now that they have a strategic and mental game plan, they feel more confident, and they are not giving away points, games, and matches. As the players in our Academy say, "I do MACH 4® first, and then I hit the ball."

MACH 4®
Mental Training System

Section One
Worksheets for Coaches and Parents

MACH 4®
Mental Training System

I
Short-Term and Long-Term Goals Worksheets

MACH ∆®

Short-Term and Long-Term Goals/Activities

MACH 4® Mental Training System: Short-Term Goals Worksheet

Date: _____

As a coach/tennis parent, what do you want your player/child to achieve within one year?

1. _____

2. _____

3. _____

What specific behaviors and actions will you do to help them achieve their short-term goals?

1. _____

2. _____

3. _____

How will you feel when they have achieved their short-term goals?

Copyright © 2008 Anne Smith, Inc. All rights reserved

MACH 4® Mental Training System:
Long-Term Goals Worksheet

Date: _____

As a coach/tennis parent, what do you want your player/child to achieve within three to five years?

1. _____

2. _____

3. _____

What specific behaviors and actions will you do to help them achieve their long-term goals?

1. _____

2. _____

3. _____

How will you feel when they have achieved their long-term goals?

Copyright © 2008 Anne Smith, Inc.   All rights reserved

MACH 4® Mental Training System:
Notes

MACH 4®
Mental Training System

II
Philosophy and Mission Statement Worksheet

MACH 4® Mental Training System:
Philosophy and Mission Statement Worksheet

Month: _____

What is your coaching/tennis parenting philosophy - what principles underlie your conduct and thoughts?

What is your coaching/tennis parenting mission statement?

What specific behaviors and actions reflect your philosophy and mission statement?

1. _____

2. _____

3. _____

Copyright © 2008 Anne Smith, Inc.　　　　　　　　　　　　　　　　　　All rights reserved

MACH 4® Mental Training System:
Notes

MACH 4®
Mental Training System

III
Emotional Goals Worksheet

MACH 4® Mental Training System: Emotional Goals Worksheet

Month: _____

What emotions make it hard for you to be a coach/tennis parent?

1. _____

2. _____

3. _____

What cues will you use to manage your emotions? (What will you say to yourself?)

1. _____

2. _____

3. _____

Copyright © 2008 Anne Smith, Inc.　　　　　　　　　　　　　　All rights reserved

MACH 4® Mental Training System:
Notes

MACH 4®
Mental Training System

IV
Body Language Goals Worksheet

MACH 4® Mental Training System: Body Language Goals Worksheet

Month: _____

What do you want to look like while coaching/watching your player/child during practices?

1. _____

2. _____

What do you want to look like while watching your player/child during matches?

1. _____

2. _____

What cues will you use to achieve your body language goals? (What will you say to yourself?)

1. _____

2. _____

Copyright © 2008 Anne Smith, Inc.   All rights reserved

MACH 4® Mental Training System:
Notes

MACH 4®
Mental Training System

V
Best Intensity Level Worksheet

MACH 4® Mental Training System:
Best Intensity Level Worksheet

Month: _____

Rate the following on a scale from 1 to 5:

What is your best intensity level during practices? _____

What is your best intensity level while talking? _____

What is your best intensity level for walking? _____

What is your best intensity level before matches? _____

What is your best intensity level during matches? _____

What is your best intensity level after matches? _____

What cues will you use to achieve your best intensity level? (What will you say to yourself?)

1. _____

2. _____

3. _____

Copyright © 2008 Anne Smith, Inc.   All rights reserved

MACH 4® Mental Training System:
Notes

MACH 4®
Mental Training System

VI
Before-Matches Worksheet

MACH 4® Mental Training System: Before-Matches Worksheet

Month: _____

What negative thoughts go through your mind before your player's/child's matches?

1. _____

2. _____

What cues will you use to manage these thoughts? (What will you say to yourself?)

1. _____

2. _____

What will you say to your player/child before their match to help them play well?

1. _____

2. _____

Copyright © 2008 Anne Smith, Inc.   All rights reserved

MACH 4® Mental Training System:
Notes

MACH 4®
Mental Training System

VII
During-Matches Worksheet

MACH 4® Mental Training System: During-Matches Worksheet

Month: _____

What negative thoughts go through your mind while watching your player's/child's matches?

1. _____

2. _____

3. _____

What cues will you use to manage those thoughts? (What will you say to yourself?)

1. _____

2. _____

3. _____

MACH 4® Mental Training System:
Notes

MACH 4®
Mental Training System

VIII
After-Matches Worksheet

MACH 4® Mental Training System:
After-Matches Worksheet

Month: _____

What negative thoughts go through your mind after your player's/child's matches (particularly the ones they lose)?

1. _____

2. _____

What cues will you use to manage those thoughts? (What will you say to yourself?)

1. _____

2. _____

What will you say to your player/child after their matches to inspire them?

1. _____

2. _____

Copyright © 2008 Anne Smith, Inc.   All rights reserved

MACH 4® Mental Training System:
Notes

MACH 4®
Mental Training System

IX
Match Summary Worksheet

MACH 4® Mental Training System:
Match Summary Worksheet

Date: _____   Opponent: _____   Score: _____

What did your player/child do well during this match?

1. _____

2. _____

3. _____

What does your player/child need to do differently in the next match?

1. _____

2. _____

3. _____

Copyright © 2008 Anne Smith, Inc.   All rights reserved

MACH 4® Mental Training System:
Notes

MACH 4®
Mental Training System

X
Progress Report Worksheet

MACH 4® Mental Training System: Progress Report Worksheet

Date: _____

What specific changes or differences do you see in your player's/child's on-court and off-court behavior since implementing MACH 4®?

1. _____

2. _____

3. _____

4. _____

What specific changes or differences do you see in your player's/child's tournament play since implementing MACH 4®?

1. _____

2. _____

3. _____

4. _____

Copyright © 2008 Anne Smith, Inc.   All rights reserved

MACH 4® Mental Training System:
Notes

MACH 4®
Mental Training System

XI
Daily Point Worksheet

MACH 4® Mental Training System: Daily Point Worksheet

Rate 1 (low) to 5 (high)

BL = Body Language   INT = Intensity   ACT = Actions

Month _____

	Drills				Points				Tournaments			+/-	Daily Total
	Footwork		Technique (Spin)		Strategy (Cross Court)		Technique (Spin)						
	BL	INT	BL	INT	BL	INT	BL	INT	BL	INT	ACT		
1													
2													
3													
4													
5													
6													
7													
8													
9													
10													
11													
12													
13													
14													
15													
16													
17													
18													
19													
20													
21													
22													
23													
24													
25													
26													
27													
28													
29													
30													
31													

Copyright © 2008 Anne Smith, Inc.   All rights reserved

MACH 4® Mental Training System:
Notes

MACH 4®
Mental Training System

XII
Match and Post-Match Intensity Level Worksheets

MACH 4® Mental Training System
Match Intensity Level Worksheet

Date: _____   Opponent: _____   Score: _____

Rate your player's/child's intensity level on serve and/or return of serve using the following scale:

1-2 = low intensity   3-4 = medium intensity   5 = high intensity

In the space to the right, rate your player's/child's intensity level on the last shot of the point using the following system:

Forehand = FH	Backhand = BH
High Forehand = HFH	Low Forehand = LFH
High Backhand = HBH	Low Backhand = LBH
Volley = FHV; BHV	Swinging Volley = SV
Overhead = OH	Approach shot = APS
Passing shot = PS	Short ball = SB
Winner = W	Ace = A
Crosscourt = CC	Down the line = DL
Return of serve = RS	Drop shot = DS
Double Fault = DF	Lob = Lob

SET SCORE: _____   SERVER: _____   OR RECEIVER: _____

GAME SCORE _____   1ST _____   2ND _____   _____

_____   1ST _____   2ND _____   _____

_____   1ST _____   2ND _____   _____

_____   1ST _____   2ND _____   _____

_____   1ST _____   2ND _____   _____

_____   1ST _____   2ND _____   _____

_____   1ST _____   2ND _____   _____

Copyright © 2008 Anne Smith, Inc.   All rights reserved

MACH 4® Mental Training System
Match Intensity Level Worksheet, Continued

_____   1ST _____   2ND _____   _____

_____   1ST _____   2ND _____   _____

_____   1ST _____   2ND _____   _____

_____   1ST _____   2ND _____   _____

_____   1ST _____   2ND _____   _____

_____   1ST _____   2ND _____   _____

_____   1ST _____   2ND _____   _____

_____   1ST _____   2ND _____   _____

_____   1ST _____   2ND _____   _____

_____   1ST _____   2ND _____   _____

_____   1ST _____   2ND _____   _____

_____   1ST _____   2ND _____   _____

_____   1ST _____   2ND _____   _____

_____   1ST _____   2ND _____   _____

_____   1ST _____   2ND _____   _____

_____   1ST _____   2ND _____   _____

_____   1ST _____   2ND _____   _____

_____   1ST _____   2ND _____   _____

_____   1ST _____   2ND _____   _____

_____   1ST _____   2ND _____   _____

MACH 4® Mental Training System
Post-Match Intensity Level Worksheet

Date: _____ Opponent: _____ Score: _____

Rate your player's/child's average intensity level for each set using the following scale:

1-2 = low intensity   3-4 = medium intensity   5 = high intensity

	1st Set	2nd Set	3rd Set
walking	_____	_____	_____
warm-up	_____	_____	_____
footwork	_____	_____	_____
ground strokes	_____	_____	_____
approach shots	_____	_____	_____
volleys/swinging volleys	_____	_____	_____
overheads	_____	_____	_____
passing shots	_____	_____	_____
return of 1st serve	_____	_____	_____
return of 2nd serve	_____	_____	_____
1st serve	_____	_____	_____
2nd serve	_____	_____	_____

Copyright © 2008 Anne Smith, Inc.   All rights reserved

MACH 4® Mental Training System:
Notes

MACH 4®
Mental Training System

XIII
Free Points & Cueing Worksheet

MACH 4® Mental Training System
Free Points & Cueing Worksheet

Date: _____   Opponent: _____   Score: _____

FREE POINTS _____   SET SCORE _____   GAME SCORE _____

FREE POINTS _____   SET SCORE _____   GAME SCORE _____

FREE POINTS _____   SET SCORE _____   GAME SCORE _____

FREE POINTS _____   SET SCORE _____   GAME SCORE _____

FREE POINTS _____   SET SCORE _____   GAME SCORE _____

OBSERVED CUES _____

OBSERVED CUES _____

OBSERVED CUES _____

OBSERVED CUES _____

OBSERVED CUES _____

OBSERVED CUES _____

Observations of opponent's comments and body language: _____

_____

_____

Copyright © 2008 Anne Smith, Inc.   All rights reserved

MACH 4® Mental Training System:
Notes

MACH 4®
Mental Training System

Section Two
Worksheets for Players

MACH 4®
Mental Training System

I
Short-Term and Long-Term Goals Worksheets

MACH 4® Mental Training System: Short-Term Goals Worksheet

Date: _____

What do you want to achieve within one year?

1. _____

2. _____

3. _____

What specific behaviors and actions will you do to achieve your short-term goals?

1. _____

2. _____

3. _____

How will you feel when you have achieved your short-term goals?

MACH 4® Mental Training System:
Long-Term Goals Worksheet

Date: _____

What do you want to achieve within three to five years?

1. _____

2. _____

3. _____

What specific behaviors and actions will you do to achieve your long-term goals?

1. _____

2. _____

3. _____

How will you feel when you have achieved your long-term goals?

Copyright © 2008 Anne Smith, Inc.   All rights reserved

MACH 4® Mental Training System:
Notes

MACH 4®
Mental Training System

II
Emotional Goals Worksheet

MACH 4® Mental Training System: Emotional Goals Worksheet

Month: _____

What emotions make it hard for you to win?

1. _____

2. _____

3. _____

What cues will you use to manage your emotions? (What will you say to yourself?)

1. _____

2. _____

3. _____

MACH 4® Mental Training System:
Notes

MACH 4®
Mental Training System

III
Body Language Goals Worksheet

MACH 4® Mental Training System: Body Language Goals Worksheet

Month: _____

What do you want to look like on the court?

1. _____

2. _____

3. _____

What cues will you use to achieve your body language goals? (What will you say to yourself?)

1. _____

2. _____

3. _____

Copyright © 2008 Anne Smith, Inc.   All rights reserved

MACH 4® Mental Training System:
Notes

MACH 4®
Mental Training System

IV
Best Intensity Level Worksheet

MACH 4® Mental Training System: Best Intensity Level Worksheet

Month: _____

Rate the following on a scale from 1 to 5:

What is your best intensity level on your forehand? _____

What is your best intensity level on your backhand? _____

What is your best intensity level on your first serve? _____

What is your best intensity level on your second serve? _____

What is your best intensity level on your volleys? _____

What is your best intensity level on your return of serve? _____

What is your best intensity level on your footwork? _____

What is your best intensity level for walking? _____

What cues will you use to achieve your best intensity level? (What will you say to yourself?)

1. _____

2. _____

3. _____

Copyright © 2008 Anne Smith, Inc.   All rights reserved

MACH 4® Mental Training System:
Notes

MACH 4®
Mental Training System

V

Cueing Language
Worksheet - Technique

MACH 4® Mental Training System: Cueing Language Worksheet Technique

Month: _____

What cues will you use on your forehand? (What will you say to yourself?)

    1. _____

    2. _____

What cues will you use on your backhand?

    1. _____

    2. _____

What cues will you use on your return of serve?

    1. _____

    2. _____

What cues will you use on your volleys?

    1. _____

    2. _____

Copyright © 2008 Anne Smith, Inc.   All rights reserved

MACH 4® Mental Training System:
Cueing Language Worksheet Technique, Continued

What cues will you use on your serve?

1. _____

2. _____

What cues will you use on your approach shots?

1. _____

2. _____

What cues will you use to help yourself be patient during the point?

1. _____

2. _____

What cues will you use to help yourself play every point the best you can?

1. _____

2. _____

MACH 4® Mental Training System:
Notes

MACH 4®
Mental Training System

VI
Game Plan Worksheet

MACH 4® Mental Training System: Game Plan Worksheet

Opponent: _____   Date: _____

What is your game plan? What is your best strategy for this match?

1. _____

2. _____

3. _____

4. _____

Score: _____

Copyright © 2008 Anne Smith, Inc.   All rights reserved

MACH 4® Mental Training System:
Notes

MACH 4®
Mental Training System

VII
Match Request Worksheet

MACH 4® Mental Training System:
Match Request Worksheet

Opponent: _____   Date: _____

What do you want your parent/coach/friends/siblings to do or say (within the rules) during your match to help you play at your best intensity level? For example, do you want them to clap or say "come on?"

1. _____

2. _____

3. _____

What do you want your parent/coach/friends/siblings to do or say after the match?

1. _____

2. _____

3. _____

Score: _____

MACH 4® Mental Training System:
Notes

MACH 4®
Mental Training System

VIII
Before-Matches Worksheet

MACH 4® Mental Training System: Before-Matches Worksheet

Month: _____

What negative thoughts go through your mind before your matches?

1. _____

2. _____

3. _____

What cues will you use to manage those thoughts? (What will you say to yourself?)

1. _____

2. _____

3. _____

Copyright © 2008 Anne Smith, Inc.   All rights reserved

MACH 4® Mental Training System:
Notes

MACH 4®
Mental Training System

IX
During-Matches Worksheet

MACH 4® Mental Training System:
During-Matches Worksheet

Month: _____

What negative thoughts go through your mind during your matches?

1. _____

2. _____

3. _____

What cues will you use to manage those thoughts? (What will you say to yourself?)

1. _____

2. _____

3. _____

Copyright © 2008 Anne Smith, Inc.   All rights reserved

MACH 4® Mental Training System:
Notes

MACH 4®
Mental Training System

X
After-Matches Worksheet

MACH 4® Mental Training System: After-Matches Worksheet

Month: _____

What negative thoughts go through your mind after your matches (particularly the ones you lose)?

1. _____

2. _____

3. _____

What cues will you use to manage those thoughts? (What will you say to yourself?)

1. _____

2. _____

3. _____

MACH 4® Mental Training System:
Notes

MACH 4®
Mental Training System

XI
Match Summary Worksheet

MACH 4® Mental Training System:
Match Summary Worksheet

Date: _____ Opponent: _____ Score: _____

What behaviors, comments, and strategies helped you to be strong and play with your best intensity level?

What behaviors, comments, and strategies caused you to **not** play with your best intensity level?

MACH 4® Mental Training System:
Notes

MACH 4®
Mental Training System

XII
Progress Report Worksheet

MACH 4® Mental Training System: Progress Report Worksheet

Date: _____

What specific changes or differences do you see in your on-court and off-court behavior since implementing MACH 4®?

1. _____

2. _____

3. _____

4. _____

What specific changes or differences do you see in your tournament play since implementing MACH 4®?

1. _____

2. _____

3. _____

4. _____

Copyright © 2008 Anne Smith, Inc.   All rights reserved

MACH 4® Mental Training System:
Notes

MACH 4®
Mental Training System

XIII
Post-Match Intensity Level Worksheet

MACH 4® Mental Training System
Post-Match Intensity Level Worksheet

Date: _____ Opponent: _____ Score: _____

Rate your average intensity level for each set using the following scale:

1-2 = low intensity   3-4 = medium intensity   5 = high intensity

	1st Set	2nd Set	3rd Set
walking	_____	_____	_____
warm-up	_____	_____	_____
footwork	_____	_____	_____
ground strokes	_____	_____	_____
approach shots	_____	_____	_____
volleys/swinging volleys	_____	_____	_____
overheads	_____	_____	_____
passing shots	_____	_____	_____
return of 1st serve	_____	_____	_____
return of 2nd serve	_____	_____	_____
1st serve	_____	_____	_____
2nd serve	_____	_____	_____

Copyright © 2008 Anne Smith, Inc.   All rights reserved

MACH 4® Mental Training System:
Notes

MACH 4®
Mental Training System

XIV
Tennis Questionnaire

MACH 4® Mental Training System Tennis Questionnaire

Date: _____ Opponent: _____ Score: _____

1. I played at my best intensity level.
   (a) not at all   (b) sometimes   (c) most of the time   (d) all of the time

2. I knew the game score and set score.
   (a) not at all   (b) sometimes   (c) most of the time   (d) all of the time

3. When my opponent's ball was out, I called "out" loudly and pointed out.
   (a) not at all   (b) sometimes   (c) most of the time   (d) all of the time

4. I used my emotions to help myself play well.
   (a) not at all   (b) sometimes   (c) most of the time   (d) all of the time

5. I used spin on my shots.
   (a) not at all   (b) sometimes   (c) most of the time   (d) all of the time

6. When it was my serve, I said the score loudly before each point.
   (a) not at all   (b) sometimes   (c) most of the time   (d) all of the time

7. I kept thinking about the shots I missed.
   (a) not at all   (b) sometimes   (c) most of the time   (d) all of the time

8. I stayed with my play patterns.
   (a) not at all   (b) sometimes   (c) most of the time   (d) all of the time

9. I displayed strong body language.
   (a) not at all   (b) sometimes   (c) most of the time   (d) all of the time

10. I used cueing language to help myself play well.
    (a) not at all   (b) sometimes   (c) most of the time   (d) all of the time

11. I did everything to help myself and not my opponent.
    (a) not at all   (b) sometimes   (c) most of the time   (d) all of the time

Copyright © 2008 Anne Smith, Inc.   All rights reserved

MACH 4® Mental Training System:
Notes

About the Author

Anne Smith, Ph.D., won her place in the history books of all-time winners with ten Grand Slam championships in doubles and mixed doubles from 1980 to 1984. She is one of only 20 women in the history of the Open Era of tennis who have won ten or more Grand Slam titles, and one of only 13 women in the Open Era to complete a career Grand Slam in women's doubles by winning at least one doubles title at all four of the majors. She has won three US Open titles, two Wimbledon titles, four French Open titles, and one Australian Open title. She was ranked No. 1 in the world in doubles in 1980 and 1981, and reached a career-high No.12 in singles in 1982. Anne went on to win the 35-and-over women's doubles at the U.S. Open and Wimbledon in 1997, and she and Stan Smith won the Champions Invitational Mixed Doubles at the U.S. Open in 2006 and 2007.

Anne has a doctorate in educational psychology with a specialization in school psychology. She is licensed to practice psychology in Arizona, Texas, and Massachusetts. Currently, Anne is a school psychologist in Arizona. She coached the World Team Tennis Boston Lobsters for three seasons, and she was the mental training consultant for Harvard University's women's tennis team in 2006 when they broke into the Top 10 for the first time and achieved their highest national ranking. Anne is the author of GRAND SLAM Coach Your Mind to Win in Sports, Business, and Life; MACH 4® Mental Training System A Handbook for Athletes, Coaches, and Parents; and MACH 4® Mental Training System Tennis Workbook.

www.ingramcontent.com/pod-product-compliance
Lightning Source LLC
Chambersburg PA
CBHW081223170426
43198CB00017B/2698